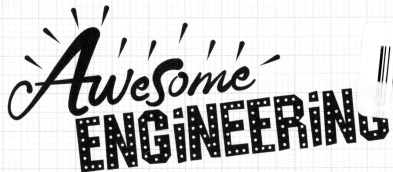

# TRAINS, PLANES, AND SHIPS

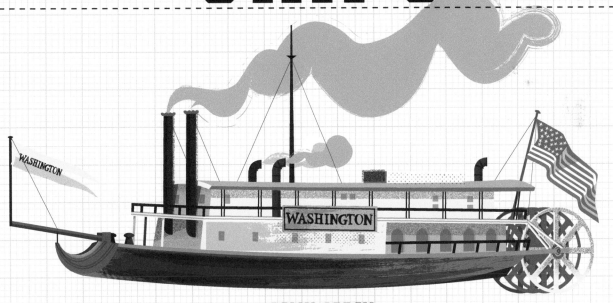

**SALLY SPRAY**

**WITH ARTWORK BY MARK RUFFLE**

CAPSTONE PRESS
a capstone imprint

Fact Finders Books are published by Capstone Press,
1710 Roe Crest Drive, North Mankato, Minnesota 56003
www.mycapstone.com

**Library of Congress Cataloging-in-Publication Data**
Library of Congress Cataloging-in-Publication data is available on the Library of Congress website.

978-1-5435-1336-3 (library binding)
978-1-5435-1342-4 (paperback)

**Editorial Credits**

Series editor: Paul Rockett
Series design and illustration: Mark Ruffle
www.rufflebrothers.com
Consultant:
Andrew Woodward BEng (Hons) CEng MICE FCIArb

**Photo Credits**

Aniza/Dreamstime: 28cl.  Azat1976/Shutterstock: 23b. Goran Cakmazovic/Shutterstock: 8b. ESB
Professional/Shutterstock: 18t. estherspoon/Shutterstock: 28r. Everett Historical/Shutterstock: 11t.
Julien Hautcoeur/Shutterstock: 13b. Philip Lange/Shutterstock: 20t. Jianhua Liang/Dreamstime:
29tc. Mandritoiu/Dreamstime: 5. Mikhail Markovskiy/Shutterstock: 29tr. Shaiful Zamri Masri/
Dreamstime: 28c. George Rinhart/Corbis Historical/Getty Images: 6. TonyV3112/Shutterstock: 26.
Konstantin Tronin/Shutterstock: 25cr. Thor Jorgen Udvang/Shutterstock: 29tl. Tao Chuen Yeh/AFP/
Getty Images: 18b.

First published in Great Britain in 2017
by The Watts Publishing Group
Copyright © The Watts Publishing Group, 2017

# TABLE OF CONTENTS

# ON THE MOVE

Trains, planes, and ships transport people and goods all over the world. This timeline highlights key moments in their evolution.

**Timeline key**

*9000 8000 7000 6000*

## BOATS

**8200–7600 BC**
The oldest boat ever found is the Pesse canoe, a dugout tree-trunk canoe found in the Netherlands.

**1550–300 BC**
The Phoenicians (who lived in modern-day Lebanon and Syria) and Greeks make wooden galley boats powered by oars.

**900 AD**
Viking longships are made from wood and are powered by oars and sails. The hulls are wide and can sail on both rivers and the sea.

**1511**
Mary Rose (see pages 6–7)

**1800s**
Tall, streamlined, sailing ships, called clippers, are used to transport cargoes of tea from China. They have many sails and are very fast.

## TRAINS

**1550s**
Rail tracks are first used to move carts carrying heavy loads. Horses or people pull the carts over rails made from wood and, later, **iron**.

**1801**
Richard Trevithick invents his first steam locomotive: the Puffing Devil. In 1804, his Penydarren locomotive is the first to run on tracks. And in 1808, the Catch-Me-Who-Can becomes the first train to carry paying passengers.

**1829**
Stephenson's Rocket (see pages 10–11)

**1829**
The Stourbridge Lion becomes the first steam engine to run in the United States. It was made in England and shipped to its new home in Pennsylvania.

**1863**
The first underground steam train system opens in London. It is called the Metropolitan Railway.

## PLANES

**c.1010**
Eilmer, a monk from Malmesbury Abbey, attaches wings to his arms and leaps from the abbey tower. According to records, he flies for 15 seconds and travels over 650 feet.

**1890**
Gustave Trouvé builds an ornithopter (a craft that flaps its wings). The wings are powered by small gunpowder explosions, and the aircraft flies for over 250 ft.

**1903**
Wright Flyer (see pages 14–15)

**1927**
Charles Lindbergh makes the first solo flight across the Atlantic in his plane the Spirit of St. Louis. This single-engined plane has an **aerodynamic** design.

**1930**
Frank Whittle invents the jet engine in Great Britain. In 1941, it was tested in the Gloster E. 28/39, the first British aircraft with a jet engine.

0

5000 4000 3000 2000 1000 1000 1100 1200 1300 1400 1500 1600 1700 1800 1900 2000

BC | AD

**1816**
Washington paddle steamer (see pages 8–9)

**1819**
SS Savannah *is the first steamship to cross the Atlantic Ocean. This wooden ship has sail power and steam-driven side paddles.*

**1843**
SS Great Britain (see pages 12–13)

**1911**
RMS *Titanic, one of the most famous ships of all time, is launched. On April 15, 1912, the enormous passenger liner sinks on its first voyage, after colliding with an iceberg.*

**2013**
USS Gerald R. Ford *aircraft carrier (see pages 26–27)*

**2015**
*The world's largest cruise ship, Harmony of the Seas, is launched. It can carry 5,479 passengers, and has a theater, climbing walls, and an ice rink!*

**1879**
*The first electric passenger locomotive is shown in Berlin. They become popular in the 1890s and are powered by a third electric rail or overhead electric cables.*

**1883**
*The Orient Express begins running between Paris and Constantinople (now Istanbul, Turkey). It offers passengers luxury travel to exotic destinations.*

**1920s**
*Diesel locomotives become widespread. They have engines that burn diesel oil to power electric motors. They are more powerful than steam trains and cause less pollution.*

**1964**
Shinkansen (bullet) train (see pages 18–19)

**2002**
Shanghai Maglev train (see pages 22–23)

**1933**
*The Boeing 247 revolutionizes air travel by providing safe, comfortable, long-distance travel for ten passengers!*

**1937**
*A* **modified** *Lockheed Electra, the XC-35, flies with a pressurized cabin, allowing people to fly without oxygen masks.*

**1939**
Heinkel He 178 (see pages 16–17)

**1969**
*The Hawker Siddeley Harrier, or Jump Jet, is the first plane able to take off vertically. It can hover and fly in any direction—even backward!*

**1969**
Concorde (see pages 20–21)

**2005**
Airbus A380 (see pages 24–25)

5

# MARY ROSE

Launched in 1511, the *Mary Rose* was part of King Henry VIII's navy. After many years of eventful service and one rebuild in 1536, the *Mary Rose* sank during the Battle of the Solent in 1545. But that was not the end of her story. In 1971, the wreck was discovered and—11 years later—was raised from the seabed.

## BUILDING BRIEF

Build a large, state-of-the-art warship to expand the Royal Navy and defend England's shores.

**Location:** Portsmouth, England

## 600 MIGHTY OAKS

The *Mary Rose* was a large **carrack** ship. Carracks are large wooden ships with tall masts and extra decks built at the bow (front) and stern (rear). The *Mary Rose* was built from high quality oak. It is estimated that more than 600 oak trees were needed to construct this mighty ship.

## STABILITY

The hull is the watertight body of the ship below the deck. The hull of the *Mary Rose* was filled with a heavy load of gravel (ballast). This kept the ship balanced and the **center of gravity** low. On its final voyage, the ship was overloaded with guns, making her top heavy. It's thought that the *Mary Rose* made a sharp turn, which caused the ship to lean. This put the **gunports** below the **waterline**, flooding the hull and causing the ship to sink.

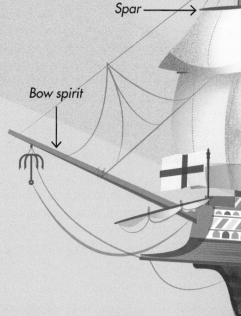

Foremast

Spar

Bow spirit

## SPEED AND STEERING

Weighing about 500 tons, the *Mary Rose* did not move quickly or easily in the water. Steering and speed were controlled by the masts and sails. Sails of different shapes and sizes caught the wind, and the wind's pressure on the sails pushed the ship along. Ropes (rigging) attached to the masts could angle the position of the sails in the direction that would best catch the wind and aid the ship's steering.

The Mary Rose was raised on a special cradle in 1982.

## CLINKER OR CARVEL?

After the ship was raised, it was possible to see which boards were original and which had been replaced during repairs in 1536. Two techniques of construction were used to build the wooden hull:

**The clinker or clench method** of shipbuilding, was older. The overlapping planks were secured by nails that were driven through the overlaps and bent over the edges. Cutting holes for guns weakened the structure.

**The carvel method** was more modern in 1536. Edge-to-edge planks were fastened to a supporting wooden frame. **Caulk** made from horsehair and thin rope filled the gaps, and a waterproof layer of tar was added.

Main mast

Triangular lateen sail

Gunports

Clinker

Carvel

Length 148 ft

# WASHINGTON PADDLE STEAMER

In the 19th century, paddle steamers became a common sight on the Mississippi River. They moved large numbers of people and vast quantities of freight, playing a significant role in the **commercial** development of the 10 states through which the river runs. The *Washington* was one of the fastest paddle steamers of all. It was launched in 1816, during the golden age of paddle power.

## BUILDING BRIEF

Design and build a ship for carrying cargo and passengers. It must be powerful enough to sail against the strong flow of the river and also stay afloat in shallow water.

**Engineer:** Henry Shreve

**Location:** Wheeling, West Virginia

## CONSTRUCTION

Constructed from wood, the bottom of the ship was flat so it could sail in shallow water. Iron rods, called hog chains, were connected to the hull at either end. Hog chains could be tightened with a **turnbuckle**. The tension in the chains made the **keel** bend downward and pressure from the water below pushed upward. These opposite **forces** kept the bottom flat.

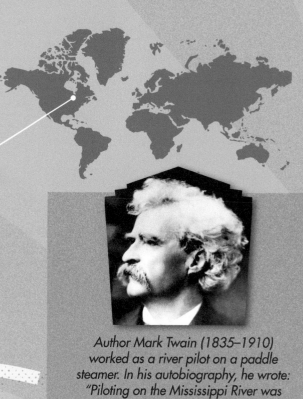

Author Mark Twain (1835–1910) worked as a river pilot on a paddle steamer. In his autobiography, he wrote: "Piloting on the Mississippi River was not work to me; it was play—delightful play, vigorous play, adventurous play—and I loved it."

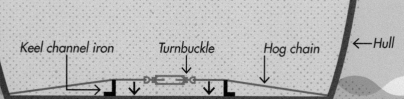

Keel channel iron · Turnbuckle · Hog chain · ←Hull

Water pressure

## STEAM POWER

The *Washington's* steam engine was positioned toward the rear of the ship, near the paddle. The fire room and boiler were positioned near the front to balance the weight of the vessel.

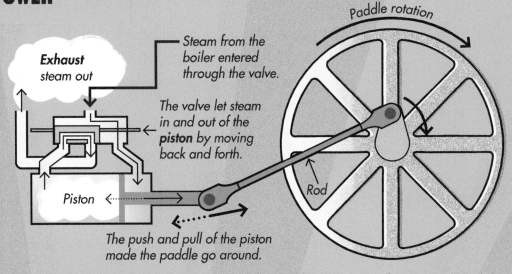

**Exhaust** steam out

Steam from the boiler entered through the valve.

The valve let steam in and out of the **piston** by moving back and forth.

Piston

The push and pull of the piston made the paddle go around.

Paddle rotation

Rod

Steam engines had just a few simple parts. A fire was lit and fed in the firebox. Heat from the fire boiled water in the boiler room. The boiled water gave off steam that was sent to a rod-and-piston **mechanism** connected to the paddle. As the steam's pressure rose, it filled the inside of the piston and moved the piston rod, which turned the paddle.

## PADDLE

The *Washington* was a sternwheeler, meaning that the single large driving paddle was at the stern of the ship. The paddle was a large wooden frame with two circles of wood at each end separated by spaced blades. When the wheel structure was turned by the engine, the blades cut into the water and scooped it backward to generate the **thrust** to move the boat along. About a quarter of the wheel entered the water at any one time.

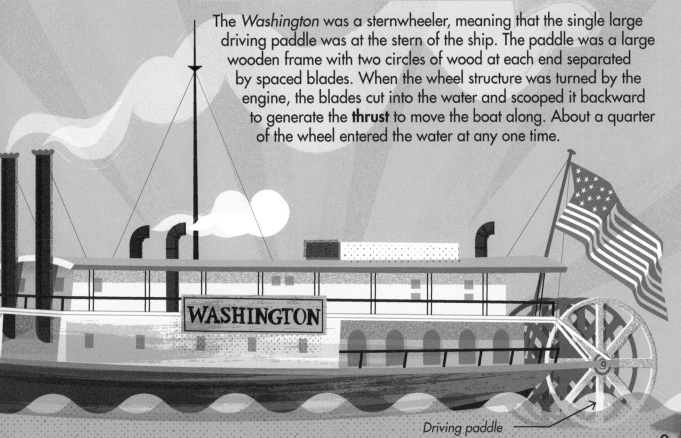

WASHINGTON

Driving paddle

Length 187 ft

# STEPHENSON'S *ROCKET*

In 1829, a competition called the Rainhill Trials was held in Merseyside, England. Its aim was to find the best steam locomotive of the day. The *Rocket* was the only locomotive to finish the trial. The prize was a contract to build steam engines to run on the Liverpool and Manchester Railway.

## BUILDING BRIEF

Design and build a reliable steam locomotive able to pull cars for freight and passengers on the newly completed railway line between Liverpool and Manchester.

**Engineers:** George Stephenson and his son Robert Stephenson

**Location:** Rainhill, Merseyside, England

# MULTI-TUBE BOILER

Earlier steam engines had just one or two pipes that carried the heat from the fire to the water tank. Instead, Stephenson's design featured a multi-tube boiler with 25 copper pipes. This allowed the water in the tank to heat up more quickly, making Stephenson's locomotive faster and more fuel-efficient.

## BLAST PIPE

*Steam out of the piston was fed into the chimney through the blast pipe. In doing so, this drew hot air out of the firebox through the pipes in the boiler. This is where the "chug-chug" of steam trains comes from as smoke and steam were blown out of the chimney with every stroke of the pistons.*

A replica of Stephenson's Rocket

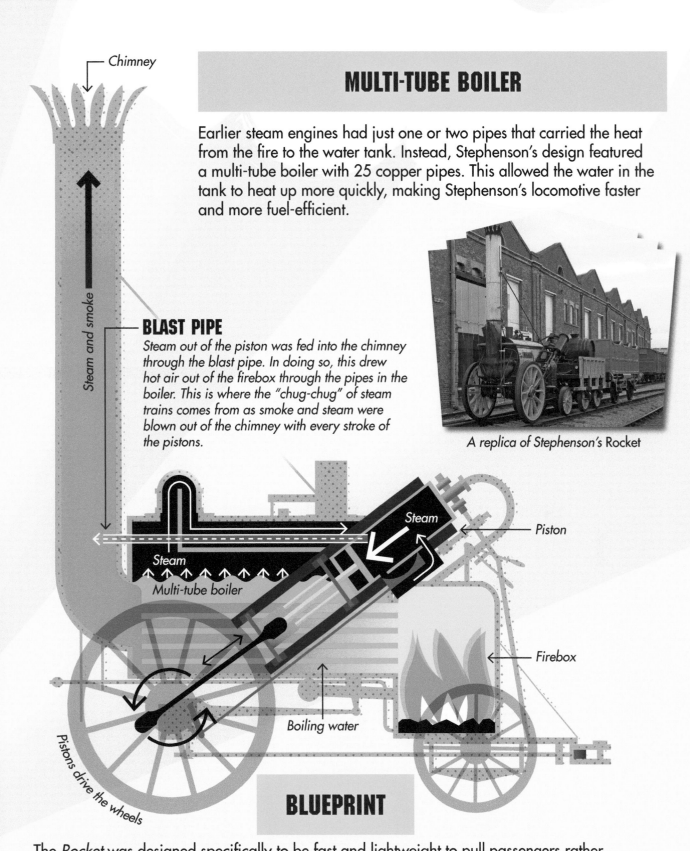

Chimney

Steam and smoke

Steam

Steam

Piston

Multi-tube boiler

Firebox

Boiling water

Pistons drive the wheels

## BLUEPRINT

The *Rocket* was designed specifically to be fast and lightweight to pull passengers rather than coal or other freight. It was not the first steam locomotive, but it was the most successful of the time, and it led to the growth of passenger railway networks. It became the **blueprint** for locomotive design for the next 150 years.

# SS *GREAT BRITAIN*

Isambard Kingdom Brunel, an **innovative** British **engineer**, brought together the most modern ideas of shipbuilding and put them all into the massive SS *Great Britain*. Launched in 1843, it was the longest passenger ship in the world at the time and the first steamship made of iron.

## BUILDING BRIEF

Build a ship using all the latest technology to carry passengers and freight across the Atlantic Ocean, between the UK and the United States.

**Engineer:** Isambard Kingdom Brunel

**Designer:** Thomas Guppy

**Location:** Bristol, England

Atlantic Ocean

*In 1845, the SS Great Britain became the first steam-powered iron ship to cross the Atlantic. The voyage took just over two weeks.*

*The SS Great Britain was powered by two enormous steam engines, but it also got an extra push from wind power. There were large sails on six iron masts that could be lowered when not in use.*

*Length 322 ft*

## IRON

At first, Brunel was going to make the SS *Great Britain*'s hull out of wood. But when he saw the *Rainbow*—an iron-hulled ship—he changed his mind. Brunel recognized that there were many advantages to using iron instead of wood:

- iron is stronger than wood and is not in danger of **dry rot** or woodworm;
- in the 19th century, iron was plentiful, while wood was expensive and harder to find for such large projects.

By the end of the planning process, the engineers had designed an enormous ship. It was 322 ft long and weighed 2,162 tons. This made it the heaviest ship in the world at the time.

*You can visit the SS* Great Britain *in Bristol, England.*

## PROPELLER POWER

On his previous ships, Brunel had used paddlewheels to push vessels through the water. This time he decided to go with a screw **propeller**. The propeller was submerged below the waterline, near the base of the hull. This position made the ship more stable in rough seas. The ship also moved through the water easier because it didn't have paddles placed on either side of the hull.

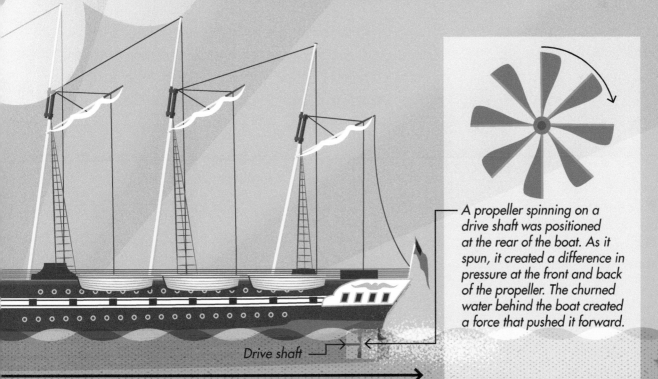

*A propeller spinning on a drive shaft was positioned at the rear of the boat. As it spun, it created a difference in pressure at the front and back of the propeller. The churned water behind the boat created a force that pushed it forward.*

Drive shaft

13

# WRIGHT FLYER

On December 17, 1903, the Wright brothers made history when their aircraft—the *Wright Flyer*—lifted off the ground. Their first flight lasted just 12 seconds and the *Wright Flyer* flew only 120 ft, but the age of powered flight had begun!

## BUILDING BRIEF

Be the first in the world to build and pilot a flying machine that can make a controlled and powered flight and change the future of modern transport.

**Engineers:** Wilbur and Orville Wright

**Location:** Kitty Hawk, North Carolina

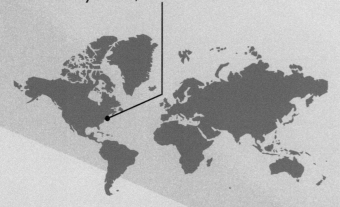

## FROM BICYCLE TO BIPLANE

Wilbur and Orville Wright had been interested in **mechanics** and engineering for most of their lives. They ran a bicycle manufacturing and repair shop and believed that cycling and flying relied on similar factors:
- the ability to balance and control the machine;
- a strong but lightweight frame;
- a **chain-and-sprocket propulsion** system;
- and a need for wind resistance and aerodynamics to increase speed.

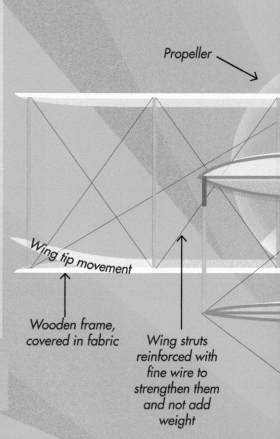

Propeller

Wing tip movement

Wooden frame, covered in fabric

Wing struts reinforced with fine wire to strengthen them and not add weight

*The* Wright Flyer *had a gas engine that powered a chain-and-sprocket device, like that on a bicycle, which linked to the two propellers.*

# TOTAL CONTROL

The success of the *Wright Flyer* was due to the very light engine and the brothers' skill at flying the plane. The different movements, known as pitch, **yaw**, and roll, could all be controlled, which allowed for a stable flight.

**ROLL**

Roll—moving the wings up or down—was controlled using a system of ropes. These allowed a twisting movement in the tips of the wings that could increase the **lift** on one wing and decrease it on the other allowing the plane to **bank**.

Yaw could be controlled using the rudder.

**YAW**

**PITCH**

Pitch—moving the nose of the plane up or down—was adjusted using the **elevator** control.

Rudder

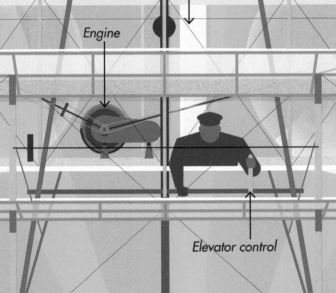

Engine

Elevator control

Wing tip movement

Chain

Sprocket

On the day of the flight, Wilbur's attempt failed, so it was Orville who made the first recorded powered flight.

# HEINKEL HE 178

The first jet-powered plane, the Heinkel He 178, flew a test flight on August 27, 1939. But it only flew for five minutes. A week later World War II began, and the inventor was forced to stop developing turbojet technology. The German airforce needed planes that could fly for much longer, so they weren't interested in the Heinkel He 178.

## BUILDING BRIEF

Be the first in the world to design and build a practical plane that could usefully harness and control the power of a jet engine.

**Engineers:** Ernst Heinkel and Dr. Hans Pabst von Ohain

**Location:** Warnemünde, Rostock, Germany

## TAKE-OFF

A plane's engine moves the plane forward quickly; this force is called thrust. Air then flows over and under the wings, causing lift. When the lift force is greater than the weight of the plane, it takes off.

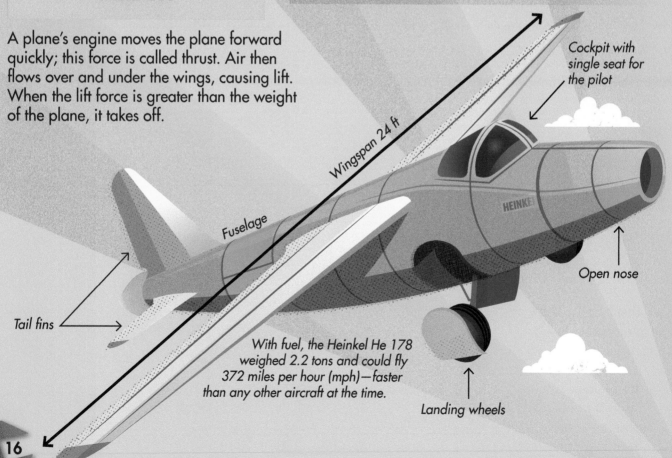

Wingspan 24 ft

Cockpit with single seat for the pilot

Open nose

Fuselage

Tail fins

With fuel, the Heinkel He 178 weighed 2.2 tons and could fly 372 miles per hour (mph)—faster than any other aircraft at the time.

Landing wheels

## DESIGN FEATURES

The Heinkel He 178 had an aerodynamic metal body that was curved for maximum **airflow**. The wings, which were wooden and curved at the ends, were fixed to the top of the fuselage (main body) behind the cockpit. It was a "tail dragger," meaning that the tail sat on the back landing wheels near the ground. The single jet engine was hidden in the middle of the plane behind the pilot. Air was taken in through the open nose to feed oxygen to the jet engine, and the high-powered exhaust fumes shot out the tail end. While the design was lightweight and sleek, flights could only last up to 10 minutes because the fuel burned so fast.

## HOW A JET ENGINE WORKS

The jet engine was invented by Sir Frank Whittle in 1930, but the design principles have changed very little since then.

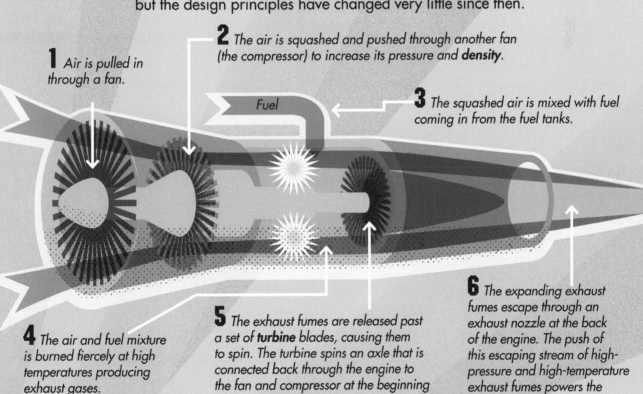

**1** *Air is pulled in through a fan.*

**2** *The air is squashed and pushed through another fan (the compressor) to increase its pressure and **density**.*

Fuel

**3** *The squashed air is mixed with fuel coming in from the fuel tanks.*

**4** *The air and fuel mixture is burned fiercely at high temperatures producing exhaust gases.*

**5** *The exhaust fumes are released past a set of **turbine** blades, causing them to spin. The turbine spins an axle that is connected back through the engine to the fan and compressor at the beginning of the engine.*

**6** *The expanding exhaust fumes escape through an exhaust nozzle at the back of the engine. The push of this escaping stream of high-pressure and high-temperature exhaust fumes powers the plane forward.*

## LATER DEVELOPMENTS

Design basics from the Heinkel He 178 were moved around to improve future aircraft. Two engines were used, one placed under each wing. This increased power and stability, making room in the fuselage for fuel tanks, which increased the flight range. The wings were also made longer, improving handling, stability, and steering.

# SHINKANSEN BULLET TRAIN

In the 1960s, Japan began work on the first rail network built for high-speed electric trains (*shinkansen* in Japanese). Now, shinkansen trains—also known as bullet trains because of their speed and appearance—zoom along tracks that link the islands of Honshu, Kyushu, and Hokkaido.

## BUILDING BRIEF

Design a new high-speed network of railways for Japan to replace the old system and help commercial development.

**Chief engineer:** Hideo Shima

**Location:** Tokyo, Japan

## BIRD BEAK

The nose shape of the Shinkansen 500 copied the tapering beak of the kingfisher bird. This aerodynamic design helped improve the train's energy consumption by around 30 percent while also reducing noise pollution.

*Kingfisher*

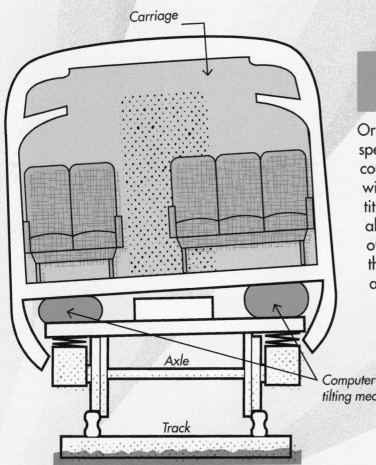

Carriage

Axle

Computer-controlled
tilting mechanism

Track

## TILTING MECHANSIM

Originally the trains had to reduce their speeds on very twisty routes because they could not turn corners at high speeds without jumping off the tracks. Then a titling mechanism was introduced that allowed the trains to lean in the direction of the turn as they sped along. This makes the ride more comfortable for passengers and keeps their drinks from falling over!

## BUZZING AXLES

Shinkansen trains are powered by an overhead electric cable. The **acceleration** and braking of each individual wheel axle is controlled by the **electric current**. This is a much lighter system than on conventional trains, where one heavy engine car pulls all the other cars and brake pads are used. The reduced weight means shinkansen trains can reach speeds over 165 mph. There is also less wear and maintenance needed on the track.

# CONCORDE

In 1969, the famous Concorde took to the skies. It was the first passenger plane to fly at a supersonic speed, which means it traveled faster than the speed of sound. In fact, the Concorde flew *twice* as fast as the speed of sound, which means you saw it coming way before you heard it.

## BUILDING BRIEF

Design and build a supersonic aircraft for super-fast passenger flights around the world.

**Engineer:** Sir James Hamilton

**Location:** London, Paris, and Bristol, England, where it was built

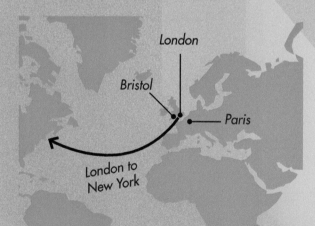

London

Bristol

Paris

London to New York

## SUPERSONIC ENGINES

The Concorde used four Rolls Royce turbojet engines, the most powerful jet engines available. They featured reheat technology, which added an extra stage in the usual jet engine process. This added more fuel to the exhaust fumes produced after the first stage of burning. This exhaust and fuel mix was burned, and the resulting superheated exhaust provided the extra thrust needed to take-off at 250 mph and to reach the supersonic cruising speed of 1,354 mph.

*The name Concorde, which means "agreement and harmony," was decided upon because the development of the project was a joint effort between Great Britain and France.*

## ARRIVE BEFORE LEAVING!

The supersonic speed of the Concorde meant that it transported passengers from London to New York in less than 3.5 hours. So in New York time, they landed an hour before they took off!

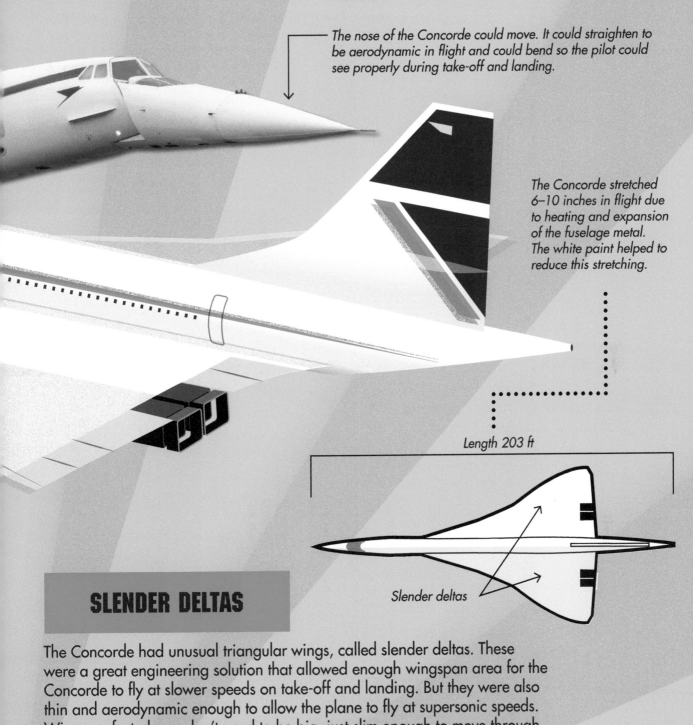

The nose of the Concorde could move. It could straighten to be aerodynamic in flight and could bend so the pilot could see properly during take-off and landing.

The Concorde stretched 6–10 inches in flight due to heating and expansion of the fuselage metal. The white paint helped to reduce this stretching.

Length 203 ft

Slender deltas

## SLENDER DELTAS

The Concorde had unusual triangular wings, called slender deltas. These were a great engineering solution that allowed enough wingspan area for the Concorde to fly at slower speeds on take-off and landing. But they were also thin and aerodynamic enough to allow the plane to fly at supersonic speeds. Wings on fast planes don't need to be big, just slim enough to move through the air and maintain lift. Lift is generated by air moving faster over the top of the wings than below them.

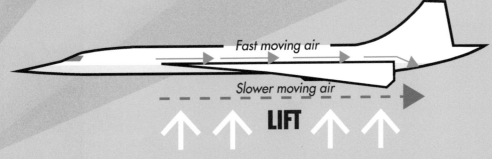

Fast moving air

Slower moving air

**LIFT**

# SHANGHAI MAGLEV TRAIN

The Shanghai Maglev Train travels just under 19 mi in each direction. But its magnetic technology means that it can whizz along at speeds over 265 mph, making it the world's fastest train.

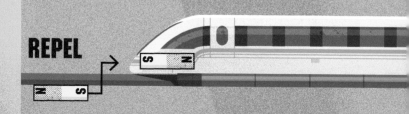

REPEL

## BUILDING BRIEF

Design and build a fast rail link between the city airport and Shanghai's metro system.

**Contractor:** Siemens

**Location:** Shanghai, China

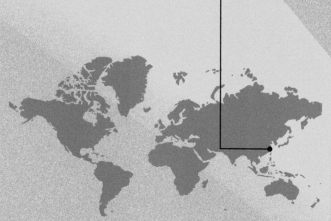

## HOW A MAGLEV WORKS

The maglev does not have any wheels. Instead it uses technology that creates an **electromagnetic** force in the track. To create this force, the system needs an electrical power source, **conductive** metal coils in the track, and magnets attached underneath and in the train. The train itself does not need an engine. When the electromagnetic force in the track is activated, it reacts against the magnets on the underside of the train. The two magnets **repel** each other, meaning they push each other away, and the train is raised, or levitated, up to 4 in above the track.

## MAGNET POWER

To understand maglev's electromagnetic technology, it helps to understand a bit about magnets. Magnets have a north pole and a south pole. If you put the north pole of one magnet and the south pole of another magnet together, they attract and come together. If you put two north poles or two south poles together, they repel and push apart.

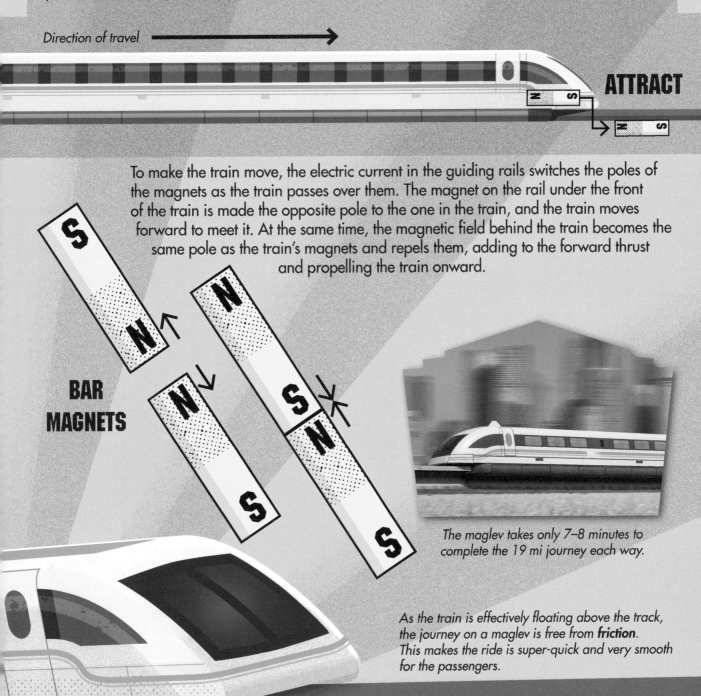

*Direction of travel*

**ATTRACT**

To make the train move, the electric current in the guiding rails switches the poles of the magnets as the train passes over them. The magnet on the rail under the front of the train is made the opposite pole to the one in the train, and the train moves forward to meet it. At the same time, the magnetic field behind the train becomes the same pole as the train's magnets and repels them, adding to the forward thrust and propelling the train onward.

**BAR MAGNETS**

*The maglev takes only 7–8 minutes to complete the 19 mi journey each way.*

*As the train is effectively floating above the track, the journey on a maglev is free from **friction**. This makes the ride is super-quick and very smooth for the passengers.*

# AIRBUS A380

The Airbus A380 is currently the largest passenger jet in service. It can carry up to 853 passengers on two levels. Despite its size, it has low **emissions** per passenger and makes less noise at take-off than many smaller planes.

## BUILDING BRIEF

Build an aircraft that is very effective at transporting large numbers of passengers long distances to reduce the cost per seat per mile traveled.

**Engineer:** Jean Roeder

**Location:** Toulouse, France

| | |
|---|---|
| —— | Barge |
| —— | Ship |
| - - - | Road |

**UK**
Broughton
Filton
Meaulte
**Germany**
Hamburg
Laupheim
Nantes
**France**
Toulouse
**Spain**
Getafe
Puerto Real

## EXHAUSTING ENGINES

Launched in 2005, the Airbus A380 is a giant of the skies. Its innovative design makes it the perfect ride for long-distance flights. It features four turbo fan engines—two on each wing—to give it the lift it needs to leave the ground. Two of the engines are fitted with thrust reversers, which on landing are used to direct engine thrust forward, rather than backward, to slow and stop the plane.

The engines can run on **kerosene** alone or a mixture of kerosene and natural gas, which means cleaner emissions.

A380

*To construct the plane, a special transport network called the Itinéraire à Grand Gabarit had to be organized. To get the large aircraft parts to Toulouse from their factories in Spain, Germany, and the United Kingdom, waterways and roads had to be widened and special barges, ships, and trucks were used.*

24

## WING TIPS

The wingspan could not be longer than 262 ft because of airport restrictions. To make up for this, the Airbus A380 has wing-tip fences at the ends, which are shaped sections pointing up and down at right angles to the wings. These allow the wings to generate more lift and reduce the **drag** placed on the aircraft, providing the benefits of a longer wing without the extra length.

The large inside space allows for more seats, or fewer seats but more luxuries. Some A380 planes have bar areas, social seating, beds, and even showers for passengers.

Wing-tip fence

Wingspan 262 ft

## MOLDING MATERIAL

Because the plane is so big, it was important to use lightweight materials that were also incredibly strong. The fuselage is made from plastic and sections of aluminum mixed with other metals.

The upper part of the fuselage is constructed using a material called GLARE®, which is made from layers of aluminum and glass fiber. GLARE® is much lighter and stronger than using metal alone and can be easily molded into an aerodynamic shape.

# USS GERALD R. FORD (CVN-78)

Aircraft carriers are phenomenal vehicles that combine sea and air power. They are also enormous—some are large enough to carry and launch up to 80 aircraft! Launched in 2013, the USS *Gerald R. Ford* is a supercarrier, the largest type of aircraft carrier. It features the most up-to-date electrical, computer, **radar**, and electromagnetic technology.

## BUILDING BRIEF

Design and build a new aircraft carrier that's able to sail for months at a time without stopping. It must provide sea and air defense for the U.S. Navy and offer better onboard living conditions.

**Builders:** Newport News Shipbuilding

**Location:** Norfolk Naval Station, Virginia (home port), USA

The radar system scans for information on different bands, putting all the readings together and displaying them on-screen. It can trace smaller and faster objects, and because it has no moving parts, it is easier to maintain.

Advances in computer technology have allowed the command center, called the island, to be smaller than on previous carriers. It is higher and nearer to the stern than earlier aircraft carriers. This allows for more flight-deck space, so aircraft can be launched and landed much more quickly.

Command center

78

# ELECTROMAGNETIC AIRCRAFT LAUNCH SYSTEM (EMALS)

Because there is not enough room on an aircraft carrier for planes to take off in the same way they do on land, a special launch system is used. The runway has a built-in track with a shuttle powered by an electromagnetic force, similar to that used on a maglev train. The aircraft is attached to the shuttle by a towbar on the front wheels. When the plane is ready to go, the engines fire up and the shuttle runs at high speed along the track, taking the plane with it and launching it off the end of the runway.

## QUICK LANDING

When a plane lands on an aircraft carrier, its tailhook snags on cables on the deck, bringing the aircraft to a quick halt. The **kinetic energy** from the plane is transferred through the **steel** cables and absorbed by them. An aircraft might come in to land at speeds over 120 mph, but it can be stopped in just two seconds!

*The tailhook underneath the plane catches on deck cables, bringing the plane to an abrupt halt.*

## POWER SURGE

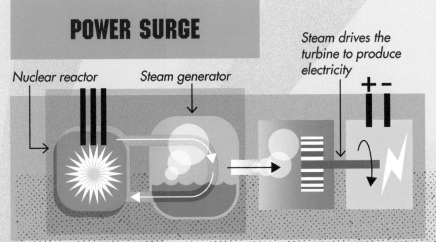

Nuclear reactor

Steam generator

Steam drives the turbine to produce electricity

Length 1,092 ft

The *Gerald R. Ford* uses a lot of electricity. To generate the power needed, the carrier has two nuclear reactors. These run off energy from **uranium**.

The uranium atoms split and cause reactions, called **fission**, within the reactor. This releases heat energy that is used to boil water, which in turn is used to drive steam turbines to generate electricity. The reactors are smaller than previous models and have fewer parts, so they require less maintenance. But they give out three times more electrical energy.

# FASCINATING FACTS

Trains, planes, and ships continue to evolve, becoming more and more awesome. Here are some additional facts about amazing engineers and terrific types of transport from around the world.

*Victoria Drummond was the first British woman to become a marine engineer. During World War II, she worked aboard ships and was commended for bravery. After the war, she worked as an engineer overseeing shipbuilding.*

## INSPIRATIONAL ENGINEERS

Many women become engineers. Here are the achievements of three pioneering women who worked on trains, planes, and ships.

*Canadian Elsie MacGill was an aeronautical engineer, meaning that she designed airplanes. Because she oversaw the mass production of Hawker Hurricane aircraft during World War II, she became know as "the Queen of the Hurricanes."*

*Olive Dennis was a railroad engineer working in the United States in the 1920s. Her job was to make rail travel more comfortable and appealing. Some of her train improvements included ceiling lights, air-conditioned compartments, and reclining seats. These comforts were adopted by rail companies and airlines all over the world.*

*The longest train ever to run was an Australian freight train. In 2001, it ran 171 mi between Newman and Port Headland. Its eight locomotives pulled 682 wagons loaded with iron ore. The train was an astonishing 4.6 mi long!*

# SOLAR POWER

Engineers are looking at new ways to power vehicles without using **fossil fuels**. Solar power is one possible solution. Solar panels gather the sun's energy and convert it into electricity or store it in batteries.

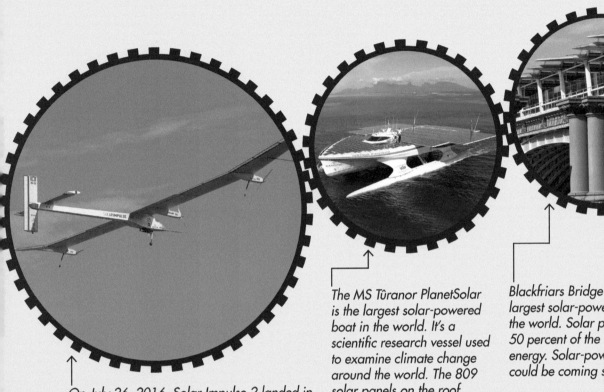

On July 26, 2016, Solar Impulse 2 landed in Abu Dhabi, completing the first around the world trip in an aircraft powered entirely by solar energy. It took 16 months to travel the incredible 26,000-mi journey.

The MS Tûranor PlanetSolar is the largest solar-powered boat in the world. It's a scientific research vessel used to examine climate change around the world. The 809 solar panels on the roof provide all the electricity that the boat needs.

Blackfriars Bridge in London is the largest solar-powered bridge in the world. Solar power provides 50 percent of the railway station's energy. Solar-powered trains could be coming soon.

One of the largest vessels in the world is the Prelude FLNG. Launched in 2013, it's a whopping 1,600 ft long. It can sail to natural gas fields, drill and extract the gas, turn it into liquid, and then carry it back to land to be used as fuel. FLNG stands for Floating Liquefied Natural Gas.

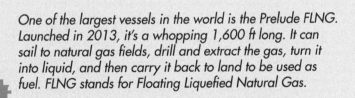

First flown in 1964, the Lockheed SR-71 Blackbird is the fastest jet ever. The Blackbird flew more than 16 mi above the ground at speeds up to 2,200 mph. It was used as a spy plane because it flew too high and too fast to be caught.

# READ MORE

Ciovacco, Justine. *All About Trains.* Let's Find Out! New York: Rosen Educational Services, 2017.

Loh-Hagan, Virginia. *Aircraft Carriers.* 21st Century Junior Library: Extraordinary Engineering. Ann Arbor, Mich.: Cherry Lake Publishing, 2017.

Roby, Cynthia. *Building Aircraft and Spacecraft: Aerospace Engineers.* Engineers Rule! New York: PowerKids Press, 2016.

Ventura, Marne. *Building Fighter Jets.* Engineering Challenges. Mendota Heights, Minn.: North Star Editions, 2017.

Verstraete, Larry. *Innovations in Transportation.* Problem Solved! Your Turn to Think Big. New York: Crabtree Publishing Company, 2017.

## INTERNET SITES

Use Facthound to find Internet sites related to this book.
Just type in 9781543513363 and go!

Check out projects, games and lots more at
**www.capstonekids.com**

# GLOSSARY

**acceleration** the change in speed of a moving object

**aerodynamic** built to move quickly and easily through the air

**airflow** the motion of air around the parts of an airplane in flight

**bank** to tilt an airplane sideways when turning

**blueprint** a diagram that shows how to construct a building or other project

**carrack** a medieval ship with three or four masts

**caulk** a waterproof paste that is applied to a hole or gap to close it and make it watertight

**center of gravity** the point at which a person's mass is evenly distributed in all directions

**chain and sprocket** a device used on bicycles that consists of a linked chain and toothed wheels (sprockets)

**commercial** suitable for business use, rather than private use

**conductive** able to convey or transmit electricity

**density** the relationship of an object's mass to its volume

**drag** the force created when air strikes a moving object; drag slows down moving objects

**dry rot** a condition in which wood is destroyed by a type of fungus

**electric current** the flow of electricity

**electromagnet** a magnet that is temporarily magnetized by an electric current

**elevator** a movable device shaped like a wing that is usually attached to the tail of an airplane for producing motion up or down

**emissions** substances released into the air by engines

**engineer** someone trained to design and build machines, vehicles, bridges, roads, or other structures

**exhaust** the waste gases produced by an engine

**fission** splitting apart of the nucleus of an atom to create large amounts of energy

**force** the push or pull on an object that results from its interaction with another object

**fossil fuels** natural fuels formed from the remains of plants and animals; coal, oil, and natural gas are fossil fuels

**friction** a force produced when two objects rub against each other; friction slows down objects

**gunport** an opening on the side of a ship through which a gun can be fired

**innovative** advanced or unlike anything done before

**iron** a hard metal used in building

**keel** the wooden or metal piece that runs along the bottom of a boat

**kerosene** a type of fuel oil made from petroleum

**kinetic energy** the energy of a moving object

**lift** the upward force of air that causes an object to fly

**mechanics** a part of science that deals with the way forces affect still or moving objects

**mechanism** a system of moving parts inside a machine

**modify** to change in some way

**piston** a disc or short cylinder within an engine that moves inside a closed tube and pushes against a liquid or a gas

**propeller** a set of rotating blades that provide the force to move an aircraft through the air

**propulsion** the forward motion of an object

**radar** a device that uses radio waves to track the location of objects

**repel** to push something away; the poles of magnets repel each other

**steel** a strong, hard metal formed from iron, carbon, and other materials

**thrust** the force that pushes a vehicle forward

**turbine** a machine with blades that can be turned by wind or a moving fluid, such as steam or water, to produce electricity

**turnbuckle** a device that is used for tightening

**uranium** a silvery-white radioactive element

**waterline** a line that marks the level of the surface of water on something: such as the hull of a ship

**yaw** to turn suddenly from a straight course

# INDEX